Dale Earnhardt Jr.

By Jeff Savage

AMAZING ATHLETES

Lerner Publications Company • Minneapolis

Lerner Publications Company
A division of Lerner Publishing Group
241 First Avenue North
Minneapolis, Minnesota U.S.A.

Website address: www.lernerbooks.com

Library of Congress Cataloging-in-Publication Data

Savage, Jeff, 1961–
    Dale Earnhardt, Jr. / by Jeff Savage.
        p.   cm. — (Amazing athletes)
    Includes index.
    ISBN-13: 978-0-8225-2946-0 (lib. bdg. : alk. paper)
    ISBN-10: 0-8225-2946-7 (lib. bdg. : alk. paper)
    1. Earnhardt, Dale, Jr.—Juvenile literature. 2. Automobile racing drivers—United States—Biography—Juvenile literature. I. Title. II. Series.
    GV1032.E18S28 2006
    796.72'092—dc22   2005003126

Manufactured in the United States of America
1 2 3 4 5 6 – DP – 11 10 09 08 07 06

TABLE OF CONTENTS

Dale Earnhardt Jr.'s number 8 *(right)* car started out as the leader at the 2004 Daytona 500. But other cars soon passed him, and he had to catch up.

A WIN FOR DAD

Dale Earnhardt Jr.'s number 8 car roared past the **grandstands** at 190 miles per hour. Thousands of fans wearing Dale's red and white colors cheered him on. Dale was racing against dozens of other drivers in the 2004 Daytona 500.

The Daytona 500 is called the Great American Race. It is the biggest and most important race of the National Association for Stock Car Automobile Racing (**NASCAR**) season. The winner of the Daytona 500 would have a great chance to win the NASCAR **points title**.

Dale was eager to win the race. But he had more than a points title on his mind. Three years earlier, Dale's father, Dale Earnhardt Sr., had been killed during the Daytona 500 race. Dale wanted to win this race for his dad.

Stock cars are like normal cars except they have bigger engines. Drivers earn points based on how they finish in races. Points are added up at the end of the season to decide the points title winner.

Dale makes a **pit stop**. His crew changes his tires and fills his car with gas.

Dale Jr. is shy and carefree. His friends and fans have given him the nickname Little E. Since his father's death, Little E has become NASCAR's most popular driver. His face appears in TV ads and on magazine covers.

On the racetrack, Dale is a tough and smart driver. In this race, he had been chasing the leader, Tony Stewart, for 30 **laps**. Dale hung close to Stewart. He waited for the perfect moment to pass.

Dale finally got his chance with less than 20 laps to go. His number 8 car came screaming out of a turn. Dale zipped high on the track to try to pass Stewart. Stewart went high to block him. Then Dale dove low. He swerved within inches of Stewart's car to move alongside it.

Dale sticks close behind number 20, Tony Stewart's car. Stewart was the leader for much of the race.

For a second, the two cars were even. Then Dale gunned his engine and roared past Stewart. The grandstands shook. "I can't believe I passed him," Dale said, "It was like a magic trick."

The crowd goes wild as Dale zips past Stewart to take the lead.

Dale zooms across the finish line as a race official waves the checkered flag. Dale has won the race!

Stewart could not catch up. Dale crossed the finish line beneath the **checkered flag**. He stopped his car and climbed out. He removed his helmet and blew a kiss to the sky. He was crying. Then he got in his car again and spun circles on the infield grass.

Finally, Dale pulled into **Victory Lane**. His **crew members** were waiting. They lifted him onto their shoulders, and the crowd roared once more. "It feels like I'm closer to Dad," said Dale. "This is the greatest day of my life."

Dale celebrates his Daytona 500 win with his teammates and friends.

Dale *(left)* with his father, Dale Earnhardt Sr. Dale Sr. was one of NASCAR's greatest drivers.

LEARNING TO RACE

Dale Earnhardt Jr. was born October 10, 1974, in Concord, North Carolina. His mother's name is Brenda Earnhardt. Dale Jr.'s parents divorced when he was three years old. So Dale and his older sister Kelley lived with their mother.

When Dale was six, a fire destroyed his mother's home. Dale and Kelley went to live with their father in Kannapolis, North Carolina. Dale also lived with his stepmother Teresa. Later, his half-brother Kerry and stepsister Taylor Nicole joined the family.

Dale Earnhardt Sr. won the Winston Cup points title seven times. He is tied for the most points title with Richard Petty.

Dale grew up around race cars and race tracks. His father was NASCAR's most popular driver. Dale Earnhardt Sr.'s tough, hard-charging style earned him the nickname the Intimidator. Dale's grandfather Ralph Earnhardt was also a top race car driver who won many races.

Dale's nickname was Junior. He loved watching races on TV.

Dale's father let his son make his own decisions. "But he always had one eye on me," Dale said. After getting his driver's license, Dale and his half-brother bought an old 1978 Chevrolet Monte Carlo for $200. They fixed the car up to race. Dale wanted to be a race car driver for one reason. "I wanted to impress my dad," he admitted.

Dale's half-brother Kerry is also a successful NASCAR driver.

Dale Sr. did not want to help his sons too much. He wanted his boys to learn about cars and racing on their own. "He's got to learn it from the bottom up," Dale Earnhardt Sr. said. "How far up he goes is based on how much he learns." Dale Jr. was not allowed to race the car until he drove it for 150 laps. One day, Dale did so without stopping. "Well," his father said, "you didn't hit anything. Let's see how you do in traffic."

It didn't take long for Dale to show he was ready to be a NASCAR driver.

A ROARING START

Dale's racing career soared from the start. He started racing when he was 17 years old. Soon he was competing at tracks in North and South Carolina.

When Dale wasn't racing, he worked at his father's car dealership. But his favorite place was the racetrack. Meanwhile, Dale's dad kept an eye on him. Dale Sr. saw that his son was an excellent driver. He thought that Dale Jr. had a chance to be a success in NASCAR.

In 1998, Dale Sr. invited his son to join his team. Dale Jr. was about to get his chance to be a NASCAR driver! He started with the **Busch Series** racing **circuit**. The Busch Series is one step below NASCAR's top circuit.

Dale was nervous during his first Busch Series race. He didn't do well. In fact, he got into a terrible crash. His car did a flip and landed on its wheels. Luckily, Dale was not hurt.

But Dale learned from his mistakes. Just two months later, he won his first Busch Series

Dale Sr. congratulates his son for winning his second Busch Series points title.

race. He earned that first victory at the Coca-Cola 300 at Texas Motor Speedway.

Dale soon won again. And again. In fact, Dale won seven races. His great season earned him the 1998 Busch Series points title. He was the champion of his circuit! It was the first time in NASCAR history that a grandfather, father, and son had all won points titles.

In 1999, Dale won six races and the Busch Series title again. Dad was proud. "He had a lot of pressure on him," said Dale Sr. "He kept his head about him. He did a good job."

Racing fans expected big things from Dale when he joined NASCAR's top circuit.

Dale joined the top level of NASCAR in 2000. He was thrilled to race against his father and the best stock car drivers in the world. He drove with a yellow stripe on the back of his number 8 car. The stripe was a sign that he was a **rookie**.

Dale soon showed that he was ready for the top NASCAR circuit. He earned his first victory in his 12th race of the season. After winning the DirecTV 500 at Texas Motor Speedway, Dale's father greeted him in Victory Lane. It was an exciting moment for both father and son.

Dale won twice more in his rookie season. He had proved his skill behind the wheel. But some people said Dale did not work hard enough at his sport. He liked to go boating and hang out with friends. "I never told anybody that I was going to be as good as my dad," said Junior. "I just want to drive race cars and make a living doing it." But then something happened that changed Dale's life forever.

Dale and his dad pose for a picture before the start of a special race at Daytona International Speedway in 2001. Dale Sr. died in a crash at Daytona just a few weeks later.

MOVING ON

Dale's life-changing moment came during the first race of the 2001 season. The 2001 Daytona 500 was a fight to the finish. On the final lap, Dale Jr. was battling Michael Waltrip for the victory. Waltrip was in first place, with Dale right behind him. Dale's father was third.

Waltrip beat out Dale for the win. But a horrible crash took place behind them. Dale Sr.'s black number 3 car had smashed into the concrete wall. Dale Sr. was killed instantly.

The racing world was shocked. NASCAR had lost its greatest driver. Dale Jr. was in shock too. In a second, he had lost his dad forever.

Dale and his stepmom Teresa get ready to speak to news reporters after Dale Sr.'s death.

Dale tried to appear strong. "We will get through this," he told reporters. "I'm sure he would want us to keep going, and that is what we are going to do."

Dale was hurting inside. But he continued to race. It was hard. Every week, fans asked him to sign pictures of his father. Before each race, NASCAR held ceremonies for Dale Sr. At the same time, TV cameras zoomed in on Dale Jr. The attention made it hard for Dale to sort out his feelings.

Fans place flowers and gifts on a Dale Earnhardt Sr. car. Racing fans around the country were shocked and saddened by Dale Sr.'s death.

Dale celebrates a victory at the Pepsi 400 at Daytona International Speedway. It was Dale's first race at Daytona since his father's death.

"The attention, the pressure, the questions . . . it had to be unbearable," said superstar racer Jeff Gordon. Gordon won the points title that year. Dale finished in eighth place. He earned $5.8 million in **prize money**.

Through it all, Dale became NASCAR's most popular driver. He was on talk shows. He made ads for car parts, razors, and rental cars. He even acted in TV shows and took batting practice at Major League Baseball's All-Star Game.

But Dale's performance did not match his popularity. In 2002, he finished in eleventh place. Early in the season, he injured his head in a crash. He drove poorly in the next several races. But Dale did not make excuses. It was time for him to do better.

Dale is strapped in and ready to race. NASCAR drivers wear helmets and special seat belts to keep them safe.

A Star Is Born

Dale grew more serious about racing. He shaved his beard and mustache. He ate healthy foods. "I want to prove there's more to me than just magazine covers and fun times," said Dale. "I think I'm a good race car driver."

Dale burns some rubber to celebrate another win.

Dale finished third in the 2003 **points standings**. He opened 2004 by winning at Daytona. And he kept on winning. At the Pontiac Performance 400 at Richmond International Raceway, Dale showed he knew how to drive like his dad. He boldly jumped on the outside of leader Jimmie Johnson and stormed past. "I'm normally not that aggressive with the car, and for just a second I felt like my daddy," said Junior. "It was kind of neat."

Dale went on to win four more races in 2004. He finished fifth in the points standings.

By 2005, Dale had earned almost $30 million in prize money for his career. He has a big collection of street cars and race cars. He also gives plenty of money to charities. Dale enjoys his life, but he is not satisfied. He wants to win a points title.

Dale battles Jeff Gordon *(left)* for the lead at the 2005 Radio Shack/ Samsung 500 at Texas Motor Speedway.

Dale's main focus is winning races, just like his father. "I don't compete against my dad's fame," Dale says. "I want to do everything I can to honor him. Part of me always wants to stay under Dad's wing. But there's a part of me that wants to break out and be my own man. I'm going to be champion. I have that confidence."

Dale gears up for another race. Racing is dangerous, but Dale doesn't worry. "I know when I go out there I could die," he says. "But if I quit driving race cars because of that, I wouldn't be living."

Selected Career Highlights

2004 Finished fifth in the Nextel Cup points standings
Won NASCAR's Most Popular Driver Award
Won the Daytona 500 at Daytona International Speedway
Won the Golden Corral 500 at Atlanta Motor Speedway
Won the Pontiac Performance 400 at Richmond International Raceway
Won the Sharpie 500 at Bristol Motor Speedway
Won the EA Sports 500 at Talladega Superspeedway
Won the Checker Auto Parts 500 at Phoenix International Raceway
Earned $8,913,510 in prize money

2003 Finished third in the Winston Cup points standings
Won Aaron's 499 at Talladega Superspeedway
Won Checker Auto Parts 500 at Phoenix International Raceway
Won NASCAR's Most Popular Driver Award
Earned $6,880,807 in prize money

2002 Finished eleventh in the Winston Cup points standings
Won Aaron's 499 at Talladega Superspeedway
Won EA Sports Thunder 500 at Talladega Superspeedway
Earned $4,970,034 in prize money

2001 Finished eighth in the Winston Cup points standings
Won the Pepsi 400 at Daytona International Speedway
Won the MBNA.com 400 at Dover Downs International Speedway
Won the Alabama 500 at Talladega Superspeedway
Earned more than $5,800,000 in prize money

2000 Finished sixteenth in the Winston Cup points standings
Won the DirecTV 500 at Texas Motor Speedway for his first Winston
  Cup victory
Won the Pontiac Excitement 400 at Richmond International Raceway
Won The Winston all-star race at Lowe's Motor Speedway
Earned $2,583,075 in prize money

1999 Won Busch Series title for second
  straight year
Won six Busch Series races

1998 Won Busch Series title
Won seven Busch Series races

Glossary

Busch Series: NASCAR's second circuit. Busch Series drivers hope to earn a spot in NASCAR's top circuit, the Nextel Cup.

checkered flag: the black-and-white flag that is waved at the end of a race

circuit: a racing league

crew members: people who build and repair NASCAR cars and trucks

grandstands: the area where fans watch a NASCAR race

laps: complete trips around a racetrack

NASCAR: the National Association for Stock Car Automobile Racing. Founded in 1947, NASCAR is the governing group of stock car racing. It says which changes to a car's engine and body are allowed to make it a stock car.

pit stop: a stop during a race in an area where a car can be fixed or gassed up

points standings: a list that shows how many points each NASCAR driver has earned. The driver with the most points is at the top of the standings. The driver with the second-most points is second in the standings and so on.

points title: an award given each year to the NASCAR driver who has earned the most points throughout the racing season. In NASCAR, drivers earn points for winning races, finishing well in races, and for other reasons.

prize money: the money awarded to each driver based on the driver's finish in a race

rookie: a first-year player or driver in a sport or league

Victory Lane: a road extending from the racetrack that the winning car drives along when celebrating a win

Further Reading & Websites

Armentrout, David, and Patricia Armentrout. *Dale Earnhardt Jr.* Vero Beach, FL: Rourke Publishers, 2004.

Gigliotti, Jim. *Dale Earnhardt Jr.: Tragedy and Triumph.* Maple Plain, MN: Tradition Books, 2004.

Kirkpatrick, Rob. *Dale Earnhardt Jr.* New York: PowerKids Press, 2002.

Stewart, Mark. *Dale Earnhardt Jr.: Driven by Destiny.* Brookfield, CT: Millbrook Press, 2003.

NASCAR.com
http://www.nascar.com
NASCAR's official site has recent news stories, driver biographies, and information about racing teams and stock cars.

The Official Website of Dale Earnhardt Jr.
http://www.dalejr.com
Dale's official website features trivia, photos, information, and occasional letters from Dale.

Sports Illustrated for Kids
http://www.sikids.com
The *Sports Illustrated for Kids* website covers all sports, including NASCAR.

Index

Photo Acknowledgments

Photographs are used with the permission of: © George Tiedemann/
NewSport/Corbis, pp. 4, 7, 26; © Michael Kim/Corbis, p. 6; © CHARLES W
LUZIER/Reuters/Corbis, p. 8; © STRINGER/USA/Reuters/Corbis, p. 9; © MARK
WALLHEISER/Reuters/Corbis, pp. 10, 20; © Reuters/CORBIS, pp. 11, 20, 21, 22,
23; © Harold Hinson/The Sporting News/ZUMA Press, p. 13; © Getty Images,
pp. 15, 25; © Brian Cleary/Icon SMI, p. 17; © Duomo/CORBIS, pp. 18, 29;
© Icon SMI/Corbis, p. 27; © JOE SKIPPER/Reuters/Corbis, p. 28.

Front cover: © Sam Sharpe/Corbis

Randal
the Elephant

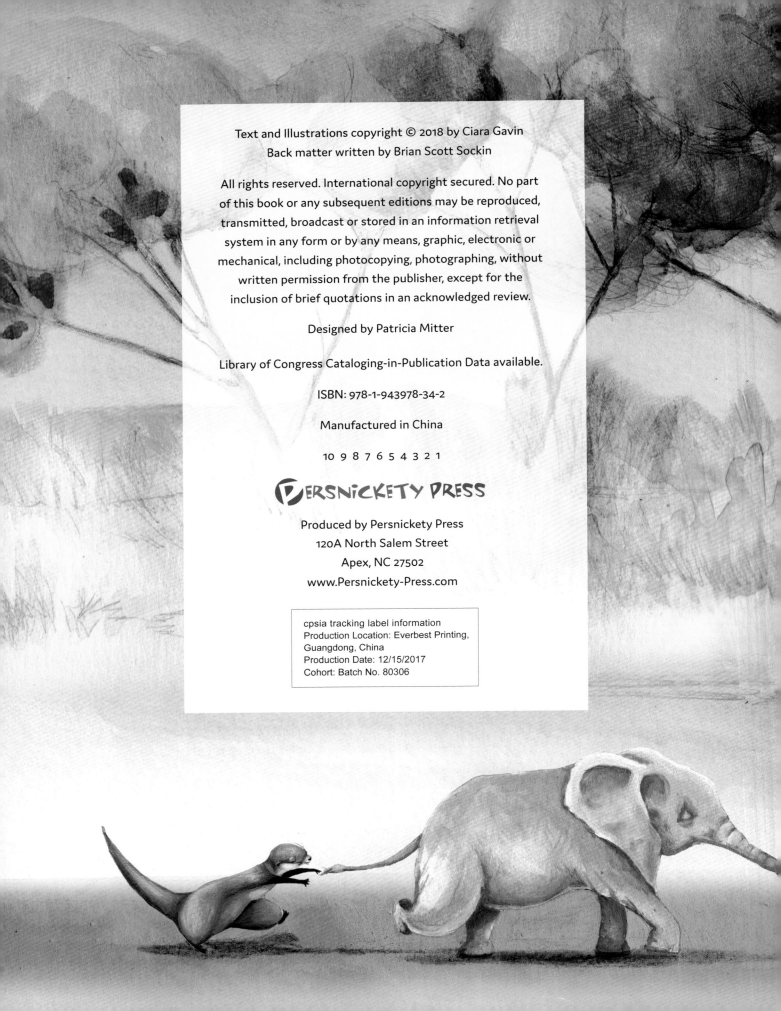

Designed by Patricia Mitter

Library of Congress Cataloging-in-Publication Data available.

ISBN: 978-1-943978-34-2

Manufactured in China

10 9 8 7 6 5 4 3 2 1

PERSNICKETY PRESS

Produced by Persnickety Press
120A North Salem Street
Apex, NC 27502
www.Persnickety-Press.com

cpsia tracking label information
Production Location: Everbest Printing,
Guangdong, China
Production Date: 12/15/2017
Cohort: Batch No. 80306

Randal
the Elephant

by Ciara Gavin

One day Randal and Clive sat watching the elephants.

"Aren't elephants majestic?" said Randal.

"Hmm, I suppose," said Clive, who wasn't too bothered with elephants.

"I heard elephants only sleep a few hours a day, which means more time for play!" said Randal.

"And elephants can take a bath with their noses. How cool is that?" he added.

"Why don't you become one?" asked Clive.

"My Mam said you can be anything you want to be. I wanted to be an otter and it's worked out just fine for me."

"How do you think I could become an elephant?"
asked Randal.

"I think you just have to spend lots of time with them and think *elephant thoughts*," said Clive.

Randal told the other otters of his plan.
Some said otters were better than elephants;
some said he should follow his dreams.

And on the day he
was ready to leave,
the otters lined
up to say goodbye.

"Best of luck Randal,"
said Clive.

After Randal left, the otters went about doing what otters do—swimming, playing, and other otter-like things.

Then one day, the otters got a letter from Randal.

Dear Clive,

I am here with the elephants,
I think they have accepted me as one of their own.
We share everything. Sometimes too much.
My trunk hasn't grown in yet but I feel very elephant on the inside.

Your friend
Randal phant

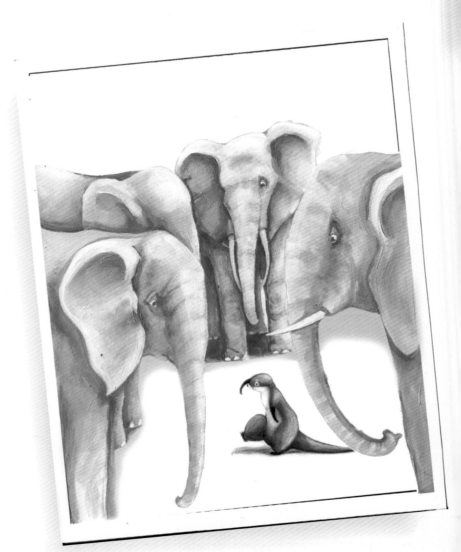

Soon after, another letter arrived...

Dear Clive

I am still here with the elephants.
They are a fun bunch. We play a game where
the pretend they dont notice me. It's really

hilarious! They are very fond of me
really or at least they will be when I become
full elephant.
　　　Yours,
　　　Randolphant

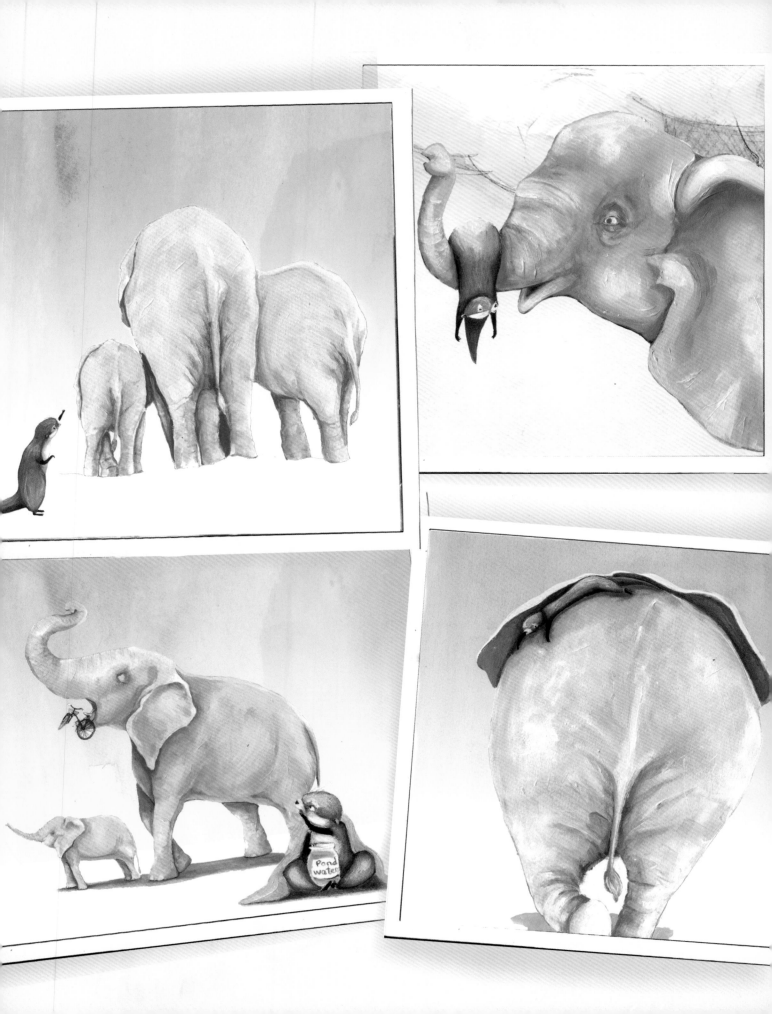

"Look! There's more on the other side!"
exclaimed Clive.

P.S. Can you please send me some
more pond water?
And pictures of the pond
and maybe some mud from the pond?

P.P.S It's not for me, it's for the
elephants.

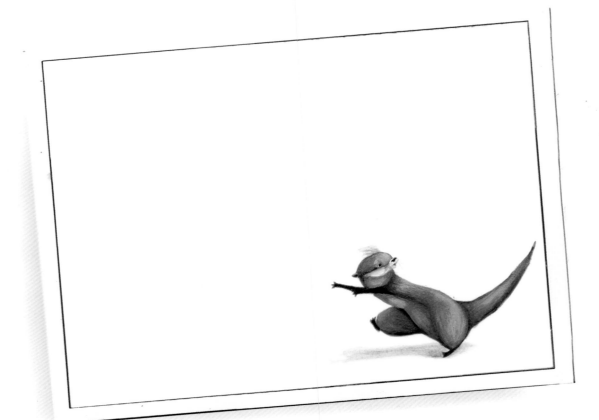

The otters thought Randal sounded happy in his new life. But the big pond wasn't the same without him.

So, they decided to go and visit him, and see if he was missing them too.

"Which one do you think is Randal?" they asked.

They picked out one that had a very *Randal* quality.

Clive walked up to him and asked, "Are you happy here Randal?"

But *Randalphant* just turned
and walked away.

"Now that he's an elephant, he probably doesn't want
to talk to otters anymore," they said sadly.

And so, they left to return
back home to the big pond.

But when they got back...

...Randal was there, waiting for them!

Randal explained that being an elephant was kinda cool, but not as great as he thought it would be.

"It's true elephants don't sleep much, but instead of more play, there was just a whole lot of sitting around," he explained.

"And everyone was so high up, I couldn't hear a word they said over the noise of their big stomping feet!" Randal added.

"I wasn't sure if I could come back," he said.
"After all, being an elephant was my dream."

"But then I remembered what Clive said, *you can be anything you want to be.*"

"And at that moment, I realized that what I REALLY wanted to be was an otter!"

"And you can change your mind as many times as you like," Clive assured him.

"Clive?" asked Randal.

"Yes, Randal," answered Clive.

"Aren't giraffes MAJESTIC?"

RANDAL WANTED TO BE AN ELEPHANT.
MAYBE THAT'S BECAUSE THEY ARE SO AMAZING!
HERE ARE SOME **COOL FACTS** ABOUT ELEPHANTS.

DID YOU KNOW?

Baby elephants suck their trunks, just like baby humans suck their thumbs!

ELEPHANTS ARE VEGETARIANS 🌿 They only eat plants and they eat a LOT of them—adults eat about 330 pounds a day!

Elephants actually **DON'T** eat peanuts!

Elephants only sleep 2 to 3 hours each day.
If people only slept that little, they'd be really tired!

Zzzz

An elephant's skin is one inch thick, but still gets hot and sunburned. That's why they cover themselves in mud!

Elephants can actually recognize themselves in the mirror. Only a few other animals besides humans are able to do that.

Elephants flap their ears to keep themselves cool.

Elephants grow new sets of teeth 6 times in their lives (humans only do this once).

Elephants can be taught to paint with a brush, like kids do in art class!

One of the ways that elephants talk to one another is by stomping their feet.

OTTERS ARE COOL, TOO!
Did you know that otters love to play?

It's fun to learn about animals and how they are alike and different from us. If you could be an animal, what would you be and why?

DIANA

Her Life in Photographs

DIANA

Her Life in Photographs

Edited by Michael O'Mara

ST. MARTIN'S PRESS

NEW YORK

DIANA: HER LIFE IN PHOTOGRAPHS

ISBN 0-312-13467-3

Designed and typeset in Monotype Bulmer
by Martin Bristow

First published in Great Britain
by Michael O'Mara Books Limited

First U.S. Edition: November 1995

10 9 8 7 6 5 4 3 2

Contents

Foreword

LADY DIANA SPENCER'S ARRIVAL on the 'public' scene as an apparently shy and blushing teenager in 1980 marked the beginning of the long, and not always requited, love affair between Diana and the camera. Even as a chubby-cheeked potential bride of Prince Charles, she somehow managed to shine when the cameras clicked. What's more, good photographs of Diana sent the sales of newspapers and magazines soaring. The result has been, over the years, literally millions of photographs taken by thousands of photographers for magazines from Tokyo to Topeka. As early as 1982, hardened professionals of the magazine industry were wondering how much longer the world's infatuation with Diana could last: A few months? A year? But Diana's popularity has confounded the pros; the normal rules of popularity simply do not seem to apply to her. Why, for instance, should the people of Peru or Indonesia take such a strong interest in a Princess from a distant land when there must be local dignitaries or beauties to catch their attention?

The answer, I believe, is glamour. The Princess provides the sort of glamour that royalty of the nineteenth century or the Hollywood of the Thirties once produced. Like a Hollywood star, Diana has made her particular glamour available to the widest possible audience through the medium of photography. But no Hollywood star ever mastered the art of looking good in photographs the way the Princess has.

Interestingly, Diana's skill before the lens is not something she was born with, as the family snaps in the opening pages of this book clearly show. As a teenager, Diana was just as awkward and uncomfortable-looking while being photographed as the rest of us. It was only after her début in public life that Diana learned to lift up her eyes and look boldly into the lens. Until her recent attempts to regain her privacy, Diana gave the impression of enormous confidence before the camera – a confidence we now know (post Andrew Morton's *Diana: Her True Story*) she could not have been feeling.

Diana's sort of beauty is the kind the camera loves best. Her features are pronounced, with deep blue eyes and a magnificent set of super-white teeth. Her training in ballet helps her to carry a long and shapely frame most elegantly. No one looks better than Diana in beautiful clothing – not even models on the catwalk.

But there is a certain indefinable quality that is the key to Diana's glamour – something that makes people care about her as a person and not just an icon. She seems to have a way of making people feel they know her personally. Whatever Diana's magic ingredient is, there is no doubt it has made her the most loved woman in the world. I hope this collection of photographs pleases Diana's many fans. I have tried to put together in one volume the very best and most important photographs of her in such a way that they would tell the story of her life. The book focuses entirely on Diana herself and does not pretend to shed any light on the ongoing drama of Britain's royal family.

MICHAEL O'MARA, 1995

1
Childhood

LEFT: *The healthy glow of country air on her cheeks, a young Diana strides out at Park House, Sandringham – the Norfolk home where she spent most of her childhood.*

BELOW: *On her first birthday, a camera-shy Diana keeps the family press at bay with a 'No pictures please' plea. Her father, the late Earl Spencer, was a keen amateur photographer.*

LEFT: *Surveying the scene from her pram – a picture taken from the family album at Park House, Sandringham. One of Diana's first memories was the smell of her plastic pram cover.*

ABOVE: *A glimpse of her spirited nature is captured by this endearing photograph of the cheeky toddler.*

11

ABOVE AND FACING PAGE ABOVE: *Diana's childhood was disrupted by the acrimonious divorce of her parents, the late Earl Spencer and Frances Shand-Kydd, when she was seven years old. Nonetheless, they ensured that she enjoyed many happy family holidays with her brother Charles and two sisters, Sarah and Jane. In 1970, she stayed at Itchenor, Sussex with her mother and her second husband, Peter Shand–Kydd.*

FACING PAGE BELOW: *Diana has always enjoyed a special bond with her brother Charles, who on the death of his father in March 1992, inherited the family title Earl Spencer. He now lives at Althorp House in Northamptonshire. He recently separated from his wife Victoria.*

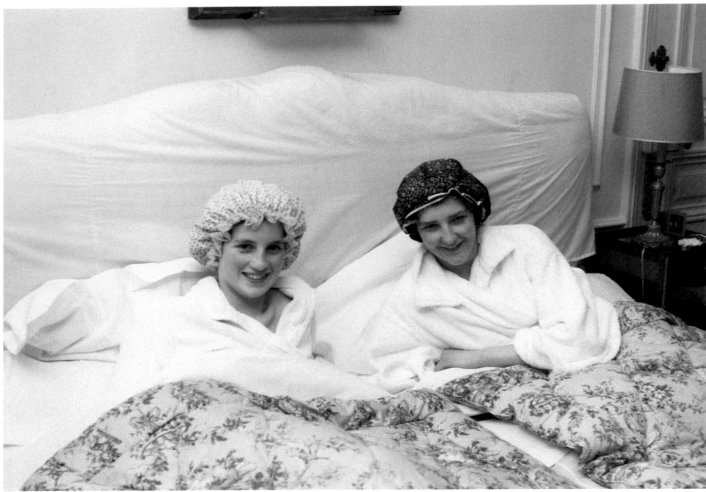

ABOVE LEFT: *The fresh-faced teenager abroad. Diana poses with her friend, Caroline Harbord-Hammond, by the banks of the river Seine in Paris, during a trip from West Heath school where she was a boarder.*

BELOW LEFT: *Relaxed and in high spirits, Diana and Caroline Harbord-Hammond clown for the camera in their bathroom attire.*

ABOVE: *A serious face on a pleasurable visit. Diana takes in the view from the top of the most famous Paris landmark, the Eiffel Tower.*

OPPOSITE ABOVE AND BELOW: *The Spencer children in a gridlock. Diana's brother Charles sits proudly at the wheel of a prized Christmas present – a blue beach buggy.*

ABOVE: *The relaxed informality of her flat-sharing days – here with Virginia Pitman – became a nostalgic dream for the young woman destined to become the Princess of Wales. Diana sits here on the roof of her Volkswagen car which she bought in 1979 and unfortunately crashed soon after.*

An athletic build enabled the streamlined Diana to win an impressive array of swimming trophies whilst a pupil at West Heath school. She even created a dive of her own – 'The Spencer Special'.

Cutting a lithe figure in her blue suit, Diana enjoyed daily swimming practice during her summer holidays. When the family moved to Althorp House, her father made a priority of installing a swimming pool for his children.

Diana has always maintained her enthusiasm for swimming. She regularly swam daily at Buckingham Palace and taught her boys, William and Harry to swim at an early age.

ABOVE: *Tennis is another love of Diana's – here playing on the private courts at Althorp House. A keen member of the exclusive Chelsea Harbour Club in London, Diana plays every day. During the annual Wimbledon tournament, she is frequently spotted in the Royal Box and has been known to snatch a game with some of the more illustrious names in the game, even playing a charity doubles match with Steffi Graf.*

ABOVE RIGHT: *The late Ruth Lady Fermoy, Diana's grandmother, was an accomplished pianist who performed in front of Queen Elizabeth, the Queen Mother at the Royal Albert Hall. Her granddaughter took lessons while at school.*

BELOW RIGHT: *Diana's step-grandmother, the romantic novelist Barbara Cartland, always gave her the latest copies of her books during visits to Althorp House.*

ABOVE: *The casually-dressed teenager learned to refine her style and dress more formally for dinner and dancing when her father entertained at Althorp.*

OPPOSITE ABOVE: *Diana has always had an instinctive rapport with children. Here with Alexandra Whitaker, her first job was as a nanny to Major Jeremy and Philippa Whitaker. She worked at their Hampshire home for three months.*

OPPOSITE BELOW: *During a visit to her mother's home in Scotland, Diana kneels alongside Soufflé, her Shetland pony. After a childhood riding accident where she broke her arm, the Princess has been a reluctant horsewoman but has encouraged her sons to ride.*

ABOVE: *Exuding self-confidence, Diana leans out of her window in a face-pack and wet towel, during a school trip.*

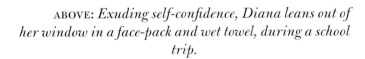

RIGHT: *Diana strikes a balletic pose in the beautiful gardens of Althorp.*

24

Despite the fact that she grew to be too tall to dance professionally, Lady Diana Spencer practised her ballet routines in the gardens at Althorp. During the colder winter months, she could be found tap-dancing her way through the black and white marble entrance hall of the house.

OPPOSITE: *The bathing beauties. With her friend Mary-Ann Stewart-Richardson, Diana sits beside one of her favourite places, the pool at Althorp House.*

LEFT: *Diana, her brother Charles and friend Mary-Ann Stewart-Richardson, relax in front of the television. These days the Princess keeps up with the long-running soap operas which gives her a useful topic for conversation when she meets the public.*

BELOW: *Her sister Sarah's legs draped over her shoulders, Diana enjoys an evening's fun with her family at Althorp.*

LEFT: *A snap of a card-game. Diana plays her hand against friend Alexandra Loyd. She was taught card games by her late grandmother, Ruth Lady Fermoy.*

BELOW: *Diana visits her brother Charles at Maidwell preparatory school, where he was a boarder.*

RIGHT: *Her right foot curled in, the embarrassment shows as a timid Diana hides behind her bobbed haircut. It is an early indication of the 'Shy Di' look which enchanted the world.*

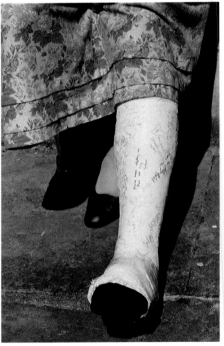

LEFT AND ABOVE: *A disastrous skiing trip left Diana's left leg encased in a plaster cast for several months. Friends and family wrote witty and sympathetic messages to Diana over the cast including Simon Berry who scribbled, 'You've been skating on thin ice lately.'*

RIGHT: *Displaying the typical nerves of a young girl, Diana poses for a photograph at Althorp House but is an unwilling model.*

LEFT: *The Spencer girls. Diana sits back-to-back with her elder sister Jane –*
someone she respects enormously and has often turned to for advice.

TOP: *Today, one of Diana's crowning glories is her trademark short blonde*
highlighted hair. When younger, her hair was light brown.

ABOVE: *With his much-prized trophy in his arms, cricketer James Cain*
carries Diana from the field after winning the match. Diana and her
friends enjoyed attending the friendly encounters between the local
village team and Althorp House.

ABOVE LEFT: *Diana takes an upside-down look at the world, while reclining on a sofa bed. She had joined a chalet party for a skiing holiday organized by her friend Simon Berry.*

BELOW LEFT: *Brotherly love from Charles. This photograph was taken by their father.*

BELOW: *Few could be immune to the attractions of Lady Diana Spencer. Certainly, Humphrey Butler, who later became an auctioneer at Christie's, looks content to have her on his knee.*

Amidst the splendour of the stately Althorp House, Diana adds her own touch of glamour
with what has now become one of her trademarks – pearls. A hint of cleavage on show,
the maturing Lady Diana Spencer poses for her father in a low-cut evening dress,
in the hallway of Althorp House before a ball in 1980.

LEFT: *In the days leading up to her wedding, Diana's hesitant glance expressed her youth and innocence, her eyes betraying the unworldliness of a girl not yet turned twenty.*

RIGHT: *Walking in Cowdray Park, Diana enjoys a chat with Sarah Ferguson, who later became her sister-in-law, the Duchess of York.*

ABOVE: *Diana at the Young England kindergarten school in Pimlico, London. This was taken in 1980 when press interest in her became intense.*

RIGHT: *Sunlight streams through Diana's flimsy summer dress, famously showing her long legs to the world. The young kindergarten teacher who had innocently posed for the photograph was mortified.*

LEFT: *Now officially engaged, Diana started to dress the part. Photographers went wild when she appeared in this daring off-the-shoulder black ballgown, worn to a charity recital at Goldsmith's Hall in London in March 1981.*

RIGHT: *Diana cuts a dash at a polo match in Windsor Park with a distinctive sheep motif jumper and red shoes. Already Diana's fashion style was in evidence.*

2
Princess

LEFT: *In a classic regal portrait, the Princess of Wales poses for photographer Lord Snowdon in 1985, effortlessly demonstrating her natural elegance and poise.*

BELOW: *Diana looks every inch the happy young mother in this official study by Tim Graham, taken only a few months after the birth of Prince William.*

ABOVE: *The early pictures of Diana show a marked difference in her facial features. In this intimate portrait by Lord Snowdon, he captures her healthy glow and plump cheeks – in contrast to later pictures where a hollow look – due to extreme weight loss – had left her gaunt and pale. Diana's battle with the slimmer's disease, bulimia, has now been well recorded and she has since spoken openly of the problems of addiction.*

RIGHT: *Patrick Lichfield took the official portraits of Diana on her wedding day on 29 July 1981. The ceremony was broadcast to 600 million people around the world.*

LEFT: *From the start, there has never been a shortage of crowds to see the Princess of Wales. Here a drenched Diana fulfils her first duties as a royal wife with a walkabout in Carmarthen, Wales. She has since recalled, 'The people who stood outside for hours and hours in the torrential rain. They were so welcoming . . . I was terrified.'*

ABOVE: *The plumpness of her bachelor days is gone. Here, having already shed several pounds since her engagement, a sylph-like Diana bares her shoulders at an official function at the Victoria and Albert Museum, London, in 1981.*

LEFT: *In 1982, just three months before the birth of Prince William, the mother-to-be radiates happiness and good health at a function at the Barbican, London.*

RIGHT: *A few months after William's birth the effects of the slimmer's disease, bulimia, were all too apparent when Diana attended the premiere of* E.T.

ABOVE: *Since her entry into the royal family, Diana has inherited and been presented with priceless jewelry, much of it given by the Queen. Here, just a year after her marriage, her youthful looks are enhanced to a more sophisticated elegance with the addition of diamonds and pearls.*

RIGHT: *Mother and son. Diana proudly shows off baby Prince William to Tim Graham's camera at Kensington Palace.*

Diana's charm and natural beauty were perfectly suited to the informal atmosphere of life in Australia. In 1983 she drew admiring glances during an official tour and is pictured here in Sydney (left) and looking soulful at Ayers Rock (right).

LEFT: *Thrilling the crowds has always been Diana's forte. She has the knack of putting people at their ease with her good humour and attention to detail. Here she responds to the electric atmosphere of well-wishers in Masterton, New Zealand.*

ABOVE: *Motherhood certainly agreed with the royal wife. Glowing with happiness, she appeared to be perfectly suited to her new royal life.*

LEFT: *The Australian Prime Minister, Malcolm Fraser encouraged Diana to bring baby William along on the 1983 tour, which meant that the royal couple were able to extend their tour by an extra two weeks to include New Zealand. Here Diana is pictured in Auckland.*

ABOVE: *Diana has always managed to combine the purity of her youthful looks with the stunning sensuality of a sophisticated woman. She keeps her make-up light and simple, allowing the richness of her jewels to add an almost ethereal look to this regal portrait.*

LEFT: *While on a royal tour of Canada, Diana celebrated her twenty-second birthday. Never short of admirers, she clutches an armful of floral gifts during a visit to Edmonton.*

ABOVE: *It was certainly a feather in Diana's cap to inspect the line-up of the Royal Newfoundland Constabulary during the tour of Canada in 1983. By now, her universal appeal was unquestioned. 'The Princess of Wales has done more to popularize the concept of monarchy throughout the world than any other member of the Royal Family in the last ten years', noted one authority.*

ABOVE: *Setting the right tone with her choice of outfits has never been a problem for the fashion-conscious Princess. During a tour of Canada, she highlighted her youthful beauty by sticking to simple, classical designs.*

RIGHT: *The Princess has never been a fan of polo, but her dazzling presence enlightened many a dull match. Here, she stands hands-on-hips at a match in Cirencester. Not a keen horsewoman herself, she has even commented to friends that, 'In another incarnation the last thing I would ever want to be is a horse.'*

LEFT: *The formal elegance of red, suits the blonde hair and blue eyes of the Princess of Wales. Shimmering in sequins and lace during a visit to Norway, she holds the camera in thrall.*

RIGHT: *Pregnant with her second child, Harry, this period of Diana's life in 1984 was one of her happiest. She had by this stage discovered from a scan that her unborn child was to be another boy.*

In 1984, Diana sported a longer, softer hairstyle. Here she is seen visiting Dr. Barnardos in the East End of London.

*Diana in Southampton – as ever, perfectly groomed for
her public duties.*

Two portraits of a modern Princess.
Delightful, fresh-faced informality (above) and dazzling,
classical regal beauty (right).

ABOVE: *The perfect English Rose.*

RIGHT: *Diana claimed on this visit to Italy in 1985 that, 'My clothes were far from my mind.' This is difficult to believe of the Princess, whose choice of attire for foreign visits has always been subtly blended with her surroundings. Here, her striking outfit was the ideal choice for a visit to the naval base at La Spezia.*

In October 1985, Diana fulfilled her role as Colonel-in-Chief of the Royal Hampshire Regiment, based in West Berlin. After inspecting the troops, she gamely donned a tracksuit and hopped into a 15-ton tank for a driving lesson.

LEFT: *Her caring nature has drawn Diana into the lives of many less fortunate and privileged people. From the homeless and mentally ill, to Aids sufferers, she has managed to reach out and embrace a huge range of needy causes. Here she flashes one of her famously therapeutic smiles for the patients at St. Joseph's Hospice in London.*

ABOVE AND BELOW: *The role she has always said she loves best – motherhood. In these two photographs taken by Tim Graham at Kensington Palace, she helps William with a jigsaw (above) and shows the two boys how to form a double act on the piano (below).*

ABOVE: *A surprise party for royal valet Ken Stronach on board the flight to Australia in 1985, brought Diana from her private quarters to join in the celebrations with her staff.*

RIGHT: *Arriving in Melbourne, Diana is in a jovial mood before disembarkation.*

LEFT: *Diana is besieged with flowers as she kneels and talks to children from Macedon, Victoria. In 1983, severe bush fires devastated the area, killing more than one hundred people.*

ABOVE: *'She would even look good in a sack', observed Princess Michael of Kent, her next door neighbour at Kensington Palace.*

THIS PAGE: *A royal visit to the USA in 1985 finds Diana in a more sombre, formal mood. At Arlington Cemetery (above) and at a function in Washington (right).*

FAR RIGHT: *When Diana attended a dinner given in honour of the royal couple by the British Ambassador and his wife in Washington, the Princess topped her beautiful, cream evening gown with this pearl and diamond tiara, a wedding gift from the Queen.*

LEFT: *Even just a glimpse of the smiling Princess through a rain-spattered window, has brought much joy to her adoring public.*

RIGHT: *Towering over her hosts, the statuesque Princess of Wales slips into a beautiful kimono, a gift from the Kimono-Makers Association in Kyoto, during a visit to Japan in 1986.*

LEFT AND ABOVE: *In the days before her separation, the Princess of Wales kept a busy diary that needed expert co-ordination and consultation. In her private sitting room at Kensington Palace, she conducts her business meetings with her current private secretary, Patrick Jephson.*

BELOW: *Designers Elizabeth and David Emanuel found favour with Diana after creating her wedding dress in 1981. They would bring fabrics and sketches to her apartment for approval. Nowadays she is more likely to visit the designer showrooms herself.*

LEFT: *At Highgrove, William and Harry have been able to enjoy the beautiful countryside and keep pets of their own. Smokey the Shetland pony was an ideal choice to initiate the young princes into the sport of riding.*

———

RIGHT: *Diana takes Prince Harry to face Tim Graham's camera in his special paratrooper's outfit.*

RIGHT: *A playful pose on the doorstep at Highgrove.*

BELOW: *Diana's pride and joy – William and Harry. Harry especially is keen on the army. His room at Kensington Palace is adorned with numerous military pictures.*

91

LEFT: *The desert Princess pictured in Oman in 1986, during a tour of the Gulf States.*

ABOVE: *'To be modern, yet keep the mystique – that is the trick', noted one observer. Diana has always been adept at mastering the two.*

Diana's life has never been plain-sailing but it has certainly presented her with exceptional challenges and excitements. Even here, preparing to fly around the Highgrove estate by helicopter, she has enjoyed a tremendously privileged view of life.

Both Diana and her sister-in-law, Sarah, Duchess of York, are keen skiers. Before they separated from their respective husbands, their friendship was especially close and Sarah's high spirits encouraged Diana to drop her formal guard on occasion. In 1987 they descended the slopes together in Klosters and clowned before the cameras.

LEFT: *Diana puts William in a spin.*

ABOVE AND RIGHT: *Diana and her two boys lend their support at polo matches, although Diana is not keen on horses herself.*

LEFT: *'In the nicest possible way, she is well aware that she is a dish', said author Clive James. With her model looks and unique sense of style, Diana is the most admired and fashionable member of the royal family since Queen Alexandra.*

ABOVE: *Diana's make-up style has remained resolutely unchanged over the years. One of her best features are her eyes which are cornflower blue and are emphasized by bright blue eyeliner. On her lips she tends to opt for natural reds and pinks, lightly glossed over.*

LEFT: *Getting used to the cameras has been made easier for the young princes after taking part in official photo calls, such as this one in Spain, where more than 60 lenses were pointed in their direction.*

RIGHT: *Three years and one day old, Prince Harry meets his new headteacher, Miss Mynor, who ran the Wetherby school in Kensington.*

LEFT: *Diana has travelled much of the world since acquiring her royal status. Here she contemplates the majestic sights of the Temple of the Emerald Buddha, in Bangkok, Thailand.*

RIGHT: *Diana, who is 5-feet-10-inches tall, mostly opts for sensibly low-heeled shoes so as not to tower over those she meets. This line-up of Australian lifeguards still manage to look almost diminutive by her side.*

LEFT: *Diana's electric presence can sometimes put others in the shade.*

ABOVE: *Viewing the sights, Thai-style, in Bangkok.*

LEFT: *A devoted mother, it has long been known that Diana yearned to have a little girl to complete her family. Here she watches Trooping the Colour with Lady Rose and Lady Davina Windsor.*

———

BELOW LEFT AND RIGHT: *The appearance of the Princess at polo matches gave rise to informal duties – presenting the prizes.*

———

RIGHT: *'Her off-duty style could be characterized as sensual masculinity', observed royal author Andrew Morton.*

LEFT: *Always supportive of British designers, Diana pays Bruce Oldfield the ultimate compliment of turning out for this Barnardos gala evening in a stunning mauve, off-the-shoulder, velvet gown. It was created by the designer, himself a former Barnardos boy.*

RIGHT: *Cool in blue, the Princess of Wales and the Duchess of York cut a dash as they leave Sandringham church in Norfolk.*

Dressing for the evening is when Diana's true beauty is really allowed to shine. Her tall, slim figure perfectly suits the intricate and sophisticated gowns she chooses to wear and she is imaginative and bold when it comes to her choice of jewelry. She often opts for fakes and has been known to alter family heirlooms.

LEFT: *Attending the Arc de Triomphe Armistice Commemoration in Paris in November 1989.*

BELOW AND RIGHT: *'Shy Di' she may have been in her early days, but once the confidence came, Diana knew how to make the most of her assets. 'The Princess of Wales knows that if clothes are going to talk, less says more', noted one fashion critic.*

*Supporting her children at their school events has always
been a priority in the Princess's diary. Nimble of foot, she
wins the Mother's Day race in 1989 at William's sports
day. Diana was thrilled: 'This is the first time in my life
I've ever won anything like this', she commented.*

Relaxing in the sun with William at a game of polo at Windsor Great Park.

Patrick Demarchelier is one of Diana's favourite photographers and these pictures were commissioned from him by British VOGUE *in 1990. He brilliantly captures both the exquisite young mother (left) and the glorious beauty of the Princess (above).*

Today, the intrusive cameras that follow Diana's every move are no longer willingly tolerated. On holiday, she can never escape the prying photographers who often go to absurd lengths to get an exclusive. Even a bike ride in the Scilly Isles (right) isn't sacred for the holidaying mum.

LEFT: *Diana observes the customs of the foreign countries she visits and during this tour of Kuwait in 1989, she obeyed the Islamic dictate of covering hair, shoulders and knees in public.*

RIGHT: *In Dubai, the blue turban-style hat encapsulates a sense of Arabia.*

A keep-fit enthusiast, Diana enjoyed the national launch of 'Bike '89' on 18 April in aid of the British Lung Foundation. Making the excuse that her skirt was too tight, she politely turned down the offer of riding one of the bicycles around the park.

A thoroughly modern mum doing the school run. Diana has a penchant for American clothing – baseball caps and cowboy boots.

RIGHT AND BELOW: *The Princess of Wales with her mother, Mrs. Frances Shand-Kydd, attend the wedding of Diana's brother, Charles to former model, Victoria Lockwood at Great Brington, near Althorp on 16 September 1990.*

FACING PAGE: *In Indonesia, Diana finds time for a quick game of bowls in front of an impressed gathering. She was visiting the Sitanala leprosy hospital on the outskirts of Jakarta.*

LEFT: *In a dazzling, beaded evening gown, Diana shimmers in her full glory at the opening ceremony for the new Hong Kong Cultural Centre on her trip to the Far East. She has been a recipient of many generous gifts of jewelry and antiques over the years and here she wears a pearl and diamond bracelet, given to her by a friend.*

RIGHT: *In Lagos, she chose a beautiful, white chiffon dress, picked out with violet flowers and green leaves, for an official function.*

LEFT: *A little crumpled in the African heat, Diana may have met her match amongst the exotic array of tribal costumes surrounding her. 'The things I do for England', she often jokes with friends, as she regales them with tales of her foreign trips.*

RIGHT: *During her visit to Nigeria in 1990, the President's wife, Mrs. Babangida, took Diana under her wing. During a ceremony, the delighted Princess received gifts from local women.*

ABOVE: *When Diana was photographed during a family holiday on the Caribbean island of Necker wearing animal-print beachwear, it instantly became a hit with all fashion-conscious women.*

RIGHT: *Her boys growing up, Diana still takes pride in doing the school trips whenever she can. Here, she takes William and Harry back for the beginning of the summer term at their preparatory school in Kensington.*

LEFT: *Film and theatre events are a great excuse to make a grand entrance. On 5 June 1990, Diana stunned onlookers in satin and lace for a charity gala evening at Sadler's Wells Theatre in London.*

RIGHT *'She is genuinely beautiful. I don't know why she needs me really', her make-up artist Barbara Daly once said.*

LEFT AND RIGHT: *Thank goodness for a sense of humour. Whatever her personal problems, Diana has kept on smiling. She knows that the public do not want to see a glum Princess.*

OVERLEAF: *Flanked by her sons, Diana heads for the mountains. Although she enjoys skiing, the tragedy in Klosters when one of their group was killed in an avalanche, left Diana understandably shaken for some time. Since her separation, she often skis with friends.*

Come rain or shine, Diana always looks beautiful and manages to make the most of every situation, even when the elements are against her.

ABOVE LEFT: *At the premiere of* Stepping Out, *Diana and film star Liza Minnelli share an intimate chat. For a time they became close friends and shared many trans-atlantic telephone conversations.*

BELOW LEFT: *A starry line-up where even Hollywood's biggest names want to meet the world's most famous royal.*

RIGHT: *Dazzling in the dark, Diana dresses in pearls and velvet in January 1992, for the Hong Kong Gala evening at the Barbican in London.*

LEFT: *A face of serenity. The Princess of Wales is lost in her private thoughts during a trip to Cairo.*

RIGHT: *Baseball cap, shorts and sneakers have always marked Diana out as an informal parent. She tries to lead as normal a life as possible when off duty, particularly when she is with her children.*

ABOVE: *On the Caribbean island of Nevis, Diana, the two boys and their friends have fun diving from their boat.*

RIGHT: *Diana enjoys shopping, particularly for her boys. Here in Cirencester, she has often been spotted popping into sweet and toy shops, stocking up with goodies.*

3
Princess Alone

LEFT: *A battery of photographers were present when the Princess attended the Headway charity event at the Hilton Hotel in December 1993. During the event, she delivered her 'resignation speech' when she appealed for herself and her children to be given 'time and space.'*

BELOW: *Despite her plea, Diana will always remain hot property for the world's press and her lone sorties through the streets of London still provide newsworthy coverage. Going from being the most famous royal in the world to being a free spirit without proper guard caused major headaches for the police.*

ABOVE: *Diana enjoys the surf with her boys.*

RIGHT: *Slowly, Diana has begun accepting more public duties again, albeit at a much reduced level. Here she attends the ISDD Media Awards lunch in London where she was presented with a special award for her successful work concerning the misuse of drugs.*

Determined to counteract the stuffiness of the Palace,
Diana continues to take her sons and their friends to
public attractions like leisure parks and fast-food bars.

*Preferring now to be left alone by the paparazzi, Diana is
more likely to be hiding behind dark glasses or running in
the opposite direction when approached by photographers
in the street.*

LEFT: *Diana in a swimsuit shows off her statuesque figure at its best. Daily work-outs and a good diet help her to keep her enviable figure.*

ABOVE: *Holidays spent at the playgrounds of the rich have attracted Diana since she has been on her own. Whether with her sons or in the company of friends, she makes sure she jets off to sunnier climes whenever she has the chance.*

LEFT: *At the New York fashion awards in 1995, Diana tried out a new look with a slicked-back hairstyle. The reactions were not altogether favourable.*

RIGHT: *Looking tanned and happy, Diana enjoys a vacation on St. Barthélemy in the Caribbean, February 1995.*

Picture Acknowledgments

Press Association: 8, 9, 10, 11, 12, 13, 23 (*bottom*)

The Late Earl Spencer's Family Album: 14, 15, 16, 17, 18, 19, 20, 21, 22, 23 (*top*), 24, 25, 26, 27, 28, 29, 30, 31, 32, 33, 34, 35, 36, 37, 38, 39

Tim Graham Picture Library: 1, 40, 41, 42, 47, 50, 51, 53, 54, 55, 56, 57, 58, 59, 60, 61, 62, 63, 64, 65, 66, 68, 69, 70, 71, 72, 73, 74, 75, 76, 77, 78, 79, 80, 81, 82, 83, 84, 85, 86, 87, 88, 89, 90, 91, 92, 93, 94, 95, 96, 99, 100, 101, 102, 103, 104, 105, 107, 108, 109, 110, 111, 112, 113, 114, 115, 116 (*top and bottom*), 117, 120, 121, 122, 123, 124, 125, 126 (*top*), 127, 128, 129, 130, 131, 132, 133, 134, 135, 136, 138, 139, 140, 141, 142 (*bottom*), 143, 144, 151, 156, 157, 159

Rex Features: 43, Scarlett Dyer

Camera Press: 2, 118, 119, Patrick Demarchelier; 44, 45, Tony Drabble; 46, 48, Snowdon; 49, Patrick Lichfield; 52, Joe Bulaitis; 126 (*bottom*), Mike Anthony; 150, Tom Wargacki

Alpha: 67, 98, Jim Bennett; 97, 106, 158, Alpha; 116 (*centre*), 145, 146, 148, 152, 153, Dave Chancellor; 137, Tim Anderson; 142 (*top*), Dave Bennett; 147, C. Postlethwaite

The Glenn Harvey Picture Collection: 149, 155